POWIS CASTLE GA

An illustrated souvenir

The National Trust

History

Gardens are very vulnerable to the changing winds of fashion, and in the eighteenth century these winds blew fierce and strong. Formal gardens fell out of favour, and many were swept away, to be replaced by open parkland, in which nature rather than man's craftsmanship was made to appear the dominant force.

Thanks to the precipitous terrain, the terraces at Powis Castle were spared this destruction, and they are the finest surviving example in Britain of a late seventeenth-century terraced garden. Although the major influences on British garden design at that time were French and Dutch, it must have been the dramatic hillside gardens of Renaissance Italy which provided the ultimate inspiration for the 'hanging gardens' of Powis.

Who the designer was and exactly when the gardens were made remains something of a mystery. The terraces were constructed during a turbulent period for the country, the castle and the Herbert family, and records have been lost. It seems most likely that work was begun in the early 1680s, when William Herbert, the 1st Marquess of Powis, was at the height of his political career. Major internal alterations were carried out to the castle at that time, probably by the architect William Winde who may also have designed the terraces. He is known to have designed a similar garden terrace at Cliveden in Buckinghamshire in the 1660s.

The Glorious Revolution of 1688 sent the Roman Catholic Marquess into exile with King James II and work on the garden presumably came to a standstill. The Marquess died in France in 1696 and the Powis estate was granted by William of Orange to his kinsman, the Earl of Rochford. But Rochford never lived at Powis and there is no evidence that he contributed to the garden.

William Herbert, 1st Marquess of Powis (1626–96), who began the construction of the terraced garden; painted c.1670

From the Wilderness ridge there are dramatic tree-framed views of the Terraces. The empty lawn and the stark red castle contrast strikingly with the richness and intricacy of the planting

Mary Preston, Marchioness of Powis (d.1724), by Michael Dahl. The wife of the 2nd Marquess, she seems to have brought over the French gardener Adrian Duval from Holland to continue the construction of the garden

We can snatch at the elusive thread again after 1703, when the Herbert family returned from exile. Included in the list of servants accompanying the wife of the 2nd Marquess from Holland was one 'Adrian Duval, native of Rouen: three months ago Lady Powis took him into her service at Ghent as a gardener. Has never been in England before.' Duval appears to have been brought to Powis, perhaps under the supervision of Winde, to continue the construction of the garden.

Writing in 1732, John Loveday records, 'Abt 30 Years since, ye Gardens were made at great expence, they have abundance of fruit. The smallest Patch, to ye front of the House, was cleared from Rock by many hands working a long time; ye lower gardens were full of wood and Rubbish; they were laid out by a Frenchman.' In 1766, the antiquary Thomas Pennant confirms this: 'The gardens are to be descended to by terraces below terraces, a laborious series of flights of steps covering rock, which one de Valle [i.e. Duval] had blasted away in former days.'

By 1705, an impressive water garden in the Dutch style had been completed on what is now the Great Lawn. 'I din'd this week at Powis Castle,' wrote John Bridgeman to his father on 8 September, 'the water-works and fountains that are finished there are much beyond anything I ever saw whose streams play near twenty yards in height the Cascade has too falls of water which concludes in a noble Bason.'

A Perspective View of Powis Castle, by Samuel and Nathaniel Buck, 1742, showing the terraced garden constructed by the 1st and 2nd Marquesses of Powis. The fountains and the rest of the Dutch-style water garden laid out on what is now the Great Lawn were dismantled at the beginning of the nineteenth century

Detail from a copy of William Marlow's painting of the North Front, *c.*1775

Pennant, his opinion reflecting the changing fashion, was less impressed. 'The gardens . . . were filled with water-works the whole in imitation of the wretched taste of St Germain-en-Laye which the late family had a most unfortunate opportunity of copying.' While in exile with James II, the 1st Marquess resided at this royal château on the Seine, west of Paris; the terraced gardens and waterworks there have since been demolished.

In 1771, William Emes was engaged by the 1st Earl of Powis, the nephew of the 3rd and last Marquess, to landscape the Park. He diverted the public road which formerly ran under the northern battlements of the castle and undertook much new planting on the Wilderness ridge beyond the Great Lawn. But by the late eighteenth century, the gardens were falling into a sorry state, thanks – according to the diarist Lord Torrington – to the 2nd Earl's indulgence 'in the prodigalities of London'. 'Not even the fruit is attended to,' he writes in 1784, 'the balustrades and terraces are falling down, and horses graze on the parterres!!!'

The 2nd Earl's successor, his brother-in-law Lord Clive, the son of the conqueror of India, brought the gardens back to 'the most complete and perfect state of repair', as, ironically, he had been instructed to do in his uncle's will, and undertook much new planting. Unfortunately, part of the improvements was the destruction, by 1809, of the baroque water garden.

Edward, 1st Earl of Powis of the third creation (1754–1839), by Hugh Douglas Hamilton. He restored the gardens and park which had been neglected by his uncle

An early nineteenth-century view of the castle, showing the enclosed deer park in the foreground

The eighteenth-century urns and shepherds on the Aviary Terrace are from the workshop of the Flemish sculptor John van Nost. All the Powis statuary has a refreshing lightness of character

Violet, Countess of Powis (1865–1929), by Ellis Roberts. She created the formal gardens to the north-east of the Great Lawn

It was Violet, wife of the 4th Earl, who instigated the next, most important period of change. In September 1911 she wrote in her journal, 'I have been anxious for several years to manage the Powis Castle garden which has been gradually deteriorating. . . It is only this year that I have been able to persuade George [her husband] to give the management over to me. And I have a great task before me. There is so much to undo, so much to do, and to plan.' Her ambition was to turn 'a poor and meagre garden' into 'one of the most beautiful, if not the most beautiful, in England and Wales'. She shared the Edwardian love of flowers and the appreciation of the formal structure of hedges, topiary and architecture, and her main contribution to the garden's design was the creation of the formal gardens to the north-east of the Great Lawn.

In the Powis tradition, this evolutionary process continues under the stewardship of the National Trust. The main change has been in the planting, which has been altered and very greatly enriched, to take full advantage of the extraordinary horticultural potential of the site and the wealth of fine plants now available. Recent improvements include the creation of a wildflower meadow to the west of the Great Lawn, and the planting of the surrounding banks with a wider range of shrubs.

The main aims are to continue to enrich and enhance the horticultural variety within the historic framework of the garden. To maintain those elements which, during the past centuries, have created this garden of great variety and individuality. Respecting the past, while embracing the present and future, will enable Lady Violet's ambition to continue in creating one of the most beautiful gardens of Wales and England (if not anywhere in the world).

Fuchsias, a favourite Edwardian plant, are a feature of Powis. Hardy varieties are planted in the borders and tender varieties are used in pots, either singly or blended with other plants

The Top Terrace

A view from the Top Terrace at dawn. The formal architecture and structural evergreens are thrown into relief by the gentle undulations of the park and Long Mountain

From the Top Terrace the spectacular panorama reveals the richness of the influences on this garden. Above you is the medieval Welsh castle, quarried from the ground where you are standing. Disappearing in layers below are the seventeenth-century Italianate terraces, overlaid with Edwardian and late twentieth-century planting. Opposite, beyond the Great Lawn, is the Wilderness ridge, first brought within the garden in the early nineteenth century. To the north-east, contained by yew hedges, is the formal garden, made after 1912. And providing the backdrop is the Powis parkland and the fertile fields, villages and great oaks of the English border countryside, backed by Long Mountain and the Breidden Hills.

Views and gardens do not always go together. Happily at Powis, the terraces are exposed only to the south-east and are protected from the prevailing winds. This allows adventurous planting on the walls and in the borders, a fact appreciated even in 1708, when sixteen shillings were paid for '2 ever green oaks, a mirtle and a pashion flower tree'. Otherwise the climate is not unusually favourable: the rainfall is comparatively low and winters can be cold. Contrary to popular belief, the terraces do not enjoy noticeably good frost drainage. The cool summers, however, promote longer flowering. The soil is rich and heavy and, with the notable exception of the Wilderness ridge, slightly alkaline in reaction.

At the west end of the terrace, beside the small rockery, the presence of *Yucca recurvifolia* has prompted a tropical theme. A wide variety of tender plants is grown, including many salvias, argyranthemums and fuchsias. Cuttings are taken in early autumn and plants are reintroduced in mid-spring. But hardier permanent plants with an exotic character are also present in the borders and on the walls behind, including *Phormium tenax, Clerodendrum bungei, Cestrum parqui* and forms of *Abutilon*.

A gigantic yew hedge marks the east end of the terraces. Emphatically stepped, but bulging contentedly, it epitomises the relaxed formality of so much of the garden

Waves of *Artemisia* 'Powis Castle' break against the wall in the centre of the Top Terrace. Each year the niches display different combinations of tender plants, devised by the Head Gardener. Here *Melianthus major* rises above fuchsias and double-flowered nasturtiums

A General Plan of Powis Castle as at present, by Thomas Farnolls Pritchard, 1771

The statue of Hercules by John van Nost against the spectacular backdrop of Powis yew

The yew topiary is a famous feature at Powis. The 14 specimen 'tumps' and the 30-foot-high hedge at the east end of the terrace were probably planted in the 1720s by the 2nd Marquess. Over the years, through changes in fashion and fortune, they have been allowed to bulge naturally and hang over the terrace walls. Sensitive pruning maintains the effect, which softens the hard lines of the architecture and gives the gardens a sense of age and plump contentment. They are trimmed each year in late summer. The darker Irish yews were planted during the following 100 years.

The pedimented niches in the wall in the centre of the terrace, formerly for the display of busts, are now used for planted containers, filled each year with different combinations of tender plants. The silver artemisia which laps the base of the wall and thrives in the dry ground above was brought here in 1972, recognised as a distinct variety, and named 'Powis Castle'. It has proved fairly hardy and happily reluctant to produce the indifferent flowers of its genus.

The lead statue at the east end of the terrace is of Hercules, fighting a stone many-headed hydra with a wooden club. The fine statues at Powis were made in the workshop of the Flemish John van Nost at the time the terraces were being created. The Hercules is signed by Andries Carpentière, one of van Nost's leading craftsmen. With the Fame and Pegasus, now in the courtyard, it probably once stood in the former water garden.

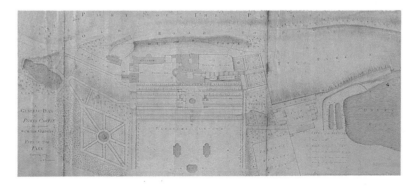

The Aviary Terrace

Descending the steps beneath an Irish Yew and ancient clump of strawberry trees, *Arbutus unedo*, you arrive at the Aviary Terrace. Fruit and vegetables were once grown here and later Hybrid Musk roses, but as the borders here are narrow and dry, it was decided to give them a Mediterranean theme and to return the banks to grass.

The patterns of silver, green and cream-variegated foliage ensure colour throughout the season, but the borders reach their flowering peak in early summer. Warm-coloured plants, including *Phlomis*, zauschnerias, brooms and Jerusalem sage, are grouped in the east border, and cool-coloured plants, such as olearias, *Rosa glauca* and *Lavatera maritima* in the west border. But throughout, the planting is softened by cistuses, blue ceanothus, and 'Bowles' Mauve' perennial wallflower.

The Aviary itself, draped in Japanese wisteria, houses a collection of deliciously scented, half-hardy rhododendrons such as 'Fragrantissimum' and 'Lady Alice Fitzwilliam'. They grow in troughs filled with acid soil and because the Aviary is unheated, polythene-covered frames are fitted over the open arches in winter. Also thriving in the cool, damp gloom are *Cestrum fasciculatum* 'Newellii', the Chain Fern (*Woodwardia radicans*), and, on the wall and roof, the creeping fig *Ficus pumila*.

The lead urns and statues of shepherds and shepherdesses are also from the workshop of John van Nost. It was fashionable to paint lead statuary in the seventeenth century, in imitation of more expensive materials or to create more life-like effects. Most of these statues were probably first painted in naturalistic colours; newly restored, they are now painted with a finish resembling weathered lead.

Japanese wisteria and white *Abutilon* frame one of the dancing shepherdesses on the Aviary Terrace

Statues line the balustrade of the Aviary Terrace

The Orangery Terrace

The Orangery Terrace is broad and level enough, and the soil deep and moist enough, for two pairs of lavishly planted herbaceous borders which are at their most spectacular in July, August and September. The hot colour theme of the east end is set by the sprawling old golden cypress, *Chamaecyparis lawsoniana* 'Lutea'. Large specimens of *Rosa moyesii* and *R. ∞ highdownensis*, which shower the borders with vermillion hips, also lend height. Among the many perennials here are macleayas, penstemons, alstroemerias, dahlias, and crocosmias, cousins of the familiar garden montbretia.

The Orangery, built to overwinter citrus fruits, is simply furnished with pots and containers and provides cool relief on hot summer days. The oranges are moved outside once fear of frost is past. The exterior walls are festooned with yellow Banksian rose and buff 'Gloire de Dijon', passion flowers and tubular-flowered eccremocarpus. The sandstone frontispiece and rusticated arch were moved here from the main entrance to the castle at the beginning of the twentieth century.

A corner of the Orangery Terrace where *Fuchsia* and *Crocosmia* infiltrate a drift of purple monkshood

Abutilon vitifolium album and the scented tea-rose 'Gloire de Dijon' flank the entrance to the Orangery

The crisp, clean lines of paths, lawn and clipped box are an ideal foil for the dramas played out in the borders

The clean lines and geometrical shapes of the paths, lawns, box hedges, and the clipped hollies flanking the statue of the Piping Faun, counter the frothing herbaceous borders in traditional Edwardian style. To aid the symmetry, the sloping bank on the west side of the Orangery is planted with *Fuchsia magellanica* 'Versicolor', which echoes in colour the flight of steps opposite. The lead figure is based on the marble Venus de' Medici in the Uffizi in Florence.

The purple hues of monkshoods, asters, thalictrums, acanthus and, on iron hoops, clematis and other climbers, link the hot and cool colour themes of these borders to east and west, resulting in an outstanding display of both colour and texture throughout.

The focal point for this walk varies with the seasons. In winter it is the tall conifers, in spring the dazzling pink foliage of *Acer pseudoplatanus* 'Brilliantissimum', and in autumn the scarlet leaves of *Euonymus alatus apterus*. Beyond the yew hedge, to the east, a lead peacock, brought from Claremont in Surrey, the home of the 1st Lord Clive, in 1931, displays against the natural quarry face, into which hypericums, aubrieta and the Mexican daisy (*Erigeron mucronatus*) have sown themselves.

The lead peacock at the west end of the Orangery Terrace

The borders at the east end of the Orangery Terrace are devoted to hot-coloured plants. Here purple clematis provide the foil for the vermilion hips of shrub roses and the reds and yellows of crocosmias and rudbeckias

Looking back to the west end of the Terraces from the South Bank. The yew hedge here marks a subtle change of mood. To the east, the garden becomes more formal, contained by hedges and punctuated by tightly clipped yews. To the west, the evergreen structure is furnished by free-growing conifers and clumps of informal shrubs

The Apple Slope and Lower Terrace

Autumn leaf colours and spring flowers are now the main features of this slope. A large concentration of Japanese maples and amelanchiers ignite the grass bank in orange and scarlet, while at the east end the unusual *Acer henryi*, one of the first to be planted in Britain after its commercial introduction in 1913, manages to mimic the mauve-pink of the Castle walls. Daffodils, primroses and colchicums grow in the grass around the trees.

The borders, overhung by *Indigofera* and *Rosa sweginzowii*, are planted for early autumn display. Chrysanthemums, asters, sedums and Japanese anemones are among the contributors; the rich purple dahlia, better known as 'Trelissick Purple' has survived more than fifteen winters here, protected only with a layer of dead magnolia leaves, which supplement the mulch.

The Box Walk

The serpentine Box Walk, leading from the east end of the Orangery Terrace, provides a gentler passage to the Formal Garden than the steps at the end of the Apple Slope Terrace. And after a feast of flower colour, the plain expanse of scented green foliage serves to rest the eye and clear the mind, while the steep descent and the height of the screening hedges (up to 20 feet) engenders a powerful sense of expectation. Like the yew, the box is cut once each year with powered hedge trimmers.

A view from the Box Walk to the Yew Walk below

The Box Walk offers cool respite from strong flower colour and leads down to the Formal Garden and Great Lawn

The Formal Garden

Golden marjoram makes a striking ground pattern beneath the vine pergola in the Formal Garden

In October 1912, the large elms which had hidden this garden – once the bowling green, then the kitchen garden – from the Castle and Terraces, were blown down in a gale. For Violet, wife of the 4th Earl, the view revealed was unacceptable. 'I am greeted every day by the repulsive sight of the detestable little [hot] houses which stare in their naked horror up at the beautiful Terraces and the grand old Castle towering above.'

She determined to turn the area into an ornamental garden. 'In my mind's eye (shall I ever see it in any other?) I see all ugliness removed. The wall removed – the grape house level with the earth: I see velvet lawns and wide paths: rose gardens – fountains – clipped yews – marble seats – herbaceous borders.'

The pyramidal fruit trees and the vine walk, the latter reputedly on the site of the former grape house, recall the earlier kitchen garden and, with the yew hedges, straight paths and post-grown roses and honeysuckles, provide the formal structure. There are a number of interesting cultivars of apple here, including 'American Mother' and 'Broad-eyed Pippin'. Beneath them, ground-cover plants tolerant of the damp heavy soil, including silver stachys and lamium, golden marjoram and black ophiopogon, serve as permanent bedding.

Rich leaf colour is evident among the trees and shrubs on the north slope of the Formal Garden, which include maples, berberis and purple cotinus. In spring, a fine specimen of *Magnolia soulangeana* 'Alexandrina' flaunts its white chalices. The most extraordinary trees are on the west slope. The spiny-stemmed, huge-leaved aralias are usually seen as suckering shrubs but conditions at Powis suit them so well that they have made single-stemmed trees over 25 feet tall. Black fruits follow the sprays of white flowers. Laburnums are also a feature on these slopes.

The garden continues to evoke the style and planting of the Edwardian era, maintaining a sense of the 'cottage garden', albeit on a lavish and extravagant scale appropriate for a countess.

Circles of silver, gold and black ground-cover plants create an equally unusual pattern beneath the Formal Garden's apple trees

The Croquet Lawn

A new yew hedge backs a pastel border of Hybrid Musk, Floribunda and modern shrub roses, underplanted with pinks and diascias, and divides the Formal Garden from the Croquet Lawn. The half-timbered Bothy, built in 1908, lends the rustic note characteristic of Edwardian gardens, though the Castle, silhouetted against the skyline and separated by ascending layers of ornamental trees and shrubs, is a constant reminder of the scale and grandeur of the Powis gardens.

The Croquet Lawn borders are planned around specific plants which give bold splashes of summer colour. Delphiniums set the theme of the walled border, succeeded in late summer by hollyhocks; the opposite border is filled with fuchsias, underplanted, for early colour, with *Geranium tuberosum*; and the remaining borders are for phlox and early Hybrid Floribunda roses, with camassias and alliums for spring.

Bowles' Wallflower with a *Ceanothus* and the rose 'Lawrence Johnson'

The delphinium border

The clipped yew doorway introduces a more domestic touch to the south-east corner of the Formal Garden

The Fountain Garden

The expression of gardening taste at Powis comes full circle in the Fountain Garden. Lady Powis introduced this simple formal water garden in the 1910s, just over 100 years after the fountains on the Great Lawn were dismantled. The wrought-iron gate, given by Lady Powis as a birthday present to her husband, is an exact copy by G. F. Bodley of the early eighteenth-century gate shown in a print of Powis House, the family's London home, demolished later in that century.

Above the gate is the Powis coat of arms, combining the Elephant of the Clives with the Griffon of the Herberts, and surmounting each pillar is a wyvern (another legendary monster) holding in its mouth a hand 'couped at the wrist', which is also on the coat of arms.

The Yew Walk and Great Lawn

Returning through the Formal Garden in the direction of the Wilderness, you pass the Yew Walk. This continues the line of the Terraces and neatly divides the Edwardian from the older garden. Like the Box Walk, it offers a pause from colour and incident.

The Great Lawn, 2½ acres in area, provides the vast empty counterweight to the imposing architecture and intricate planting above, and, from all sides, is a smooth foil for the ridges and distant hills opposite.

Fuchsias in a basketweave pot

Detail of a bright Powis border

The wrought-iron gates are based on those which once stood outside the family's London home, Powis House

One of the clipped box bushes in the Fountain Garden

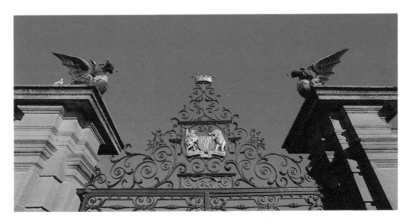

The Wilderness

The Wilderness offers a change of mood from the formal patterns of the Terraces and Edwardian gardens, and gives dramatic views of the Castle ridge and border countryside. Woodland walks were enjoyed here in the early eighteenth century, and much new planting was undertaken by William Emes after 1771. The Wilderness was brought into the garden and the deer fenced out in the nineteenth century, and the older exotic trees date from that period.

Oaks grow to enormous sizes at Powis and are the dominant trees in the Wilderness, with yews forming the evergreen understorey. Other notable trees here include fine specimens of tulip tree, small-leaved lime, *Nothofagus procera*, and handkerchief trees (*Davidia involucrata*). Among the best conifers are wellingtonia and *Cryptomeria japonica*.

Remarkably, the Wilderness ridge is formed of acid rock, in contrast to the palaeozoic limestone of the parallel Castle ridge. This enabled the 3rd Earl to participate in the nineteenth-century fashion for lime-hating rhododendrons. Large clumps of *R. ponticum* and the scented yellow azalea (*R. luteum*) paint the wooded walks in spring, and many interesting species and hybrids have since been added to extend the colour range and flowering season. Bluebells, snowdrops and wildflowers also contribute. The range of shrubs has been widened in recent years to include hydrangeas, viburnums, dogwoods, magnolias and many others, reducing the territory of the invasive *R. ponticum*.

The Plunge Bath on the lower walk is a Victorian addition; it requires a leap of faith today to imagine that at one time our forbears might have plunged themselves into these waters for invigorating purposes. The Ice House on the west edge of the Wilderness probably dates from the early nineteenth century; it was recently rescued from the undergrowth and restored. The path leads over a wooden bridge constructed from Montgomeryshire oak.

The Stable Pond

The Stable Pond, on the west tip of the Wilderness crescent and almost outside the garden proper, is now the only sizeable expanse of water at Powis. It is informally edged with rushes, royal fern and giant-leaved gunnera; note how *Acanthus spinosus* is successfully battling with the invasive wild heliotrope. There are some fine conifers here including, near the road, *Pinus monticola*, and, on the opposite bank, *Abies nordmanniana*.

A view through the trees in the Wilderness

The large stone Patagon foot was sculpted by Vincent Woropay in the form of a colossal fragment. It was bought in 1987 for Powis with the help of the Matthew Prichard Settlement and others

The Daffodil Paddock

Across the bridge and down the bank is a sweep of meadow, separated from the Great Lawn by a yew hedge. A succession of flowers appear in the grass from spring until high summer, including wild daffodils, primroses, buttercups, yellow-rattle, orchids and a variety of grasses. Many occur here naturally but many have been introduced as young plants, including astrantia and trollius. The meadow receives its first cut at the beginning of August and is mown regularly thereafter. Bamboos, sorbaria, and coppiced willows and dogwoods also thrive in the wet ground.

The Western Bank

The Daffodil Paddock affords an excellent view of the diverse collection of trees and shrubs on the Western Bank. There is a high concentration of conifers among them, including an impressive twin-stemmed *Chamaecyparis nootkatensis* 'Pendula', and these make a visual link with the evergreens on the Terraces beyond. As you walk up the slope, you will also encounter beautiful specimens of paperbark maple, *Eucryphia ∞ nymansensis* 'Nymansay', a very tall maidenhair tree, and a splendid old sycamore, with partly exposed roots.

The ambition of Violet, Countess of Powis, was to turn her 'poor and meagre garden' into 'one of the most beautiful, if not the most beautiful, in England and Wales.' Scenically dramatic, lavishly planted and layered in history, the Powis Castle garden is today recognised as being of the highest horticultural and historical importance, and the National Trust employs seven full-time gardeners, assisted by part-time helpers and trainees, to maintain it. But like all good gardens, it is forever changing, subtly day by day, spectacularly season by season, and we hope you will come again soon to see these changes for yourself.

The daffodil paddock in April

Powis offers the unusual opportunity to view borders from a variety of angles – from above, from below, and even from the Wilderness ridge opposite. The horizontal lines of the terraces are kept exposed, but here and there a plant rises from the terrace below or tumbles from the terrace above